THE SAYINGS OF THE GREAT RELIGIOUS LEADERS

Editor: Andrew Linzey

The Sayings of Jesus

Selected by Andrew Linzey
Director of the Centre for the Study of Theology in the University of Essex

The Sayings of Moses

Selected by Dan Cohn-Sherbok
University Lecturer in Jewish Theology in the University of Kent

The Sayings of Muhammad

Selected and Translated by Neal Robinson
Senior Lecturer in Religious Studies in the Cheltenham and Gloucester College of Higher Education

The Sayings of the Buddha

Selected by Geoffrey Parrinder
Emeritus Professor of Comparative Study of Religions in the University of London, King's College

The Sayings of

THE
BUDDHA

selected by
GEOFFREY PARRINDER

DUCKWORTH

First published in 1991 by
Gerald Duckworth & Co. Ltd.
The Old Piano Factory
43 Gloucester Crescent, London NW1 7DY

Introduction and editorial arrangement
© 1991 by Geoffrey Parrinder

All rights reserved. No part of this publication
may be reproduced, stored in a retrieval system, or
transmitted, in any form or by any means, electronic,
mechanical, photocopying, recording or otherwise,
without the prior permission of the publisher.

ISBN 0 7156 2374 5

British Library Cataloguing in Publication Data
The Sayings of the Buddha.
1. Theravada Buddhism. Scriptures
I. Buddha   II. Parrinder, Geoffrey *1910–*
294.3823

ISBN 0-7156-2374-5

Photoset in North Wales by
Derek Doyle & Associates, Mold, Clwyd
Printed in Great Britain by
Redwood Press Limited, Melksham

Contents

7 Introduction
12 Family and Renunciation
13 The Four Signs
15 Search and Enlightenment
17 The Four Noble Truths
19 The Noble Eightfold Path
20 The Middle Way
21 The Marks of Not-Self
24 The Buddha
28 The Doctrine
30 The Order
33 Women, Nuns
35 Lay Followers
37 Social Classes
39 Social Duties
41 Karma
43 Rebirth
45 Nirvana
47 Meditation
48 Faith
49 Austerities
51 Miracles
53 After Death
54 Chief Gods
57 Decline and Renewal
59 Debates
60 Ten Open Questions
61 Last Days

Introduction

The Buddha was one of the greatest teachers of humanity, revered for over two thousand years by millions in Asia, and today many people in all continents are interested in his teachings. Like some other religious teachers, the Buddha never wrote a book, and the many sayings and stories attributed to him were written down by early or later followers. Even more than with the Gospels, these teachings came from the early community, though there seems to be much of the imprint of his personality on them.

The scriptures of the more conservative southern Buddhists, the Theravada (or Hinayana), followers of the Teaching of the Elders, are several times the length of the Bible. Scribes used the phrase 'thus have I heard', but they developed traditions if they thought they could be improved. These scriptures were composed over several centuries and the oldest existing manuscript, a version of the short Dhamma-pada, 'virtue path', dates from the first or second century AD.

The man whom we call *the* Buddha is believed to have been one in a long series. There are references to past Buddhas, and hope of a Buddha to come, Maitreya, but our Buddha is the only one of this present world era of about half a million years. The name Buddha is a title meaning the 'Enlightened' or 'Awakened', comparable to the title Christ, 'Anointed'. His personal name was Siddhartha but it is rarely used. More frequent was Gautama (or Gotama), the family name, or he might be given the clan title, Shakya-muni, 'the sage of the Shakyas'.

Several titles are used in the scriptures. One is Bhagava, meaning 'exalted', teacher, Master, or Lord. More obscure is Tathagata, which may have been derived from words for 'thus come' or 'thus gone', which seems to be 'one who has come and gone like former Buddhas'. I have generally rendered such titles as Master or Buddha, the latter especially after his enlightenment.

Buddhism has often been called agnostic or even

atheistic by modern western writers, and it did reject or ignore many of the popular Indian gods. Some of them – Brahma, Sakra (Indra) and the tempter Mara – appear in the Buddhist scriptures, but they are inferior to the Buddha. He himself was not called a god, indeed that would be unworthy, since the gods are still caught up in the round of rebirths. But the Buddha is above them all, called 'Teacher of gods and men'. In function for the believer he is the Supreme Being, and from early years Buddhists confessed, 'I go to the Buddha for refuge', as Hindus went to Krishna or Shiva for refuge.

With the Buddha there is the Doctrine or Truth (Dharma or Dhamma), and the Order (Sangha). Dharma is a complex term: doctrine, teaching, law, norm, virtue, righteousness, religion, truth. The Doctrine is not simple morality or a system of self-improvement. It is a revelation of eternal truth from the omniscient Buddha and transmitted by experts in the Order.

At first the Order may have indicated the whole community of believers, but it came to denote particularly the inner circles of dedicated monks. They were not enclosed in fortress monasteries but wandered freely through the world, while seeking detachment from its lusts and follies. The Order has been the inner church of Buddhism, though today it has been attacked or abolished in some countries and the future of Buddhism there depends on the lay followers.

The dates of the Buddha are uncertain. Southern Buddhists have one tradition that his death occurred in the sixth century BC, and others would put it about a hundred years before the great Buddhist emperor Ashoka who ruled over much of India from about 270 BC. Many scholars place the Buddha's dates at 563-483 BC, though probably the fifth or fourth century is near enough.

He was born in northern India, or the foothills of Nepal, to a princely family. Thus he belonged to the Rajah warrior-ruler caste or class, and not to the Brahmin priestly class of the Hindu religion, and rivalries between the classes appear in the texts. Traditional sites for the Buddha's birth, enlightenment and death have been revered and the emperor Ashoka had monuments placed there. It is said that Siddhartha was married and had a child, and then at the age of twenty-nine he renounced his home to take up the homeless life in search of a solution to the problems of suffering. Eventually he was 'enlightened' – became Buddha – under a sacred pipal tree, said to be the Bo-tree at Gaya in modern Bihar.

From Gaya the Buddha went to the sacred city of Benares or Varanasi, and in a deer park at Sarnath he preached his first sermon, setting out the basic Four Noble or Aryan Truths, and the way to achieve peace by the Noble Eightfold Path. The site of this first teaching is still marked by the lofty remains of a monument erected by Ashoka.

For some fifty years the Buddha and his followers wandered round northern India teaching. He finally died at Kusinara, which the texts call a 'wattle-and-daub town in the midst of the jungle', no doubt thinking that he should have passed away in a great city like Benares. But the memory of the humble location supports the truth of the story. He had already attained Nirvana, the extinction of all craving, at his enlightenment, and now he entered Parinirvana, complete Nirvana.

In this selection traditional accounts of the Buddha's family and enlightenment are put first and his death last, to provide a framework for the sayings. They are nearly all said to have come from the Buddha himself, though no doubt given form by later scribes. The ensuing sayings and stories appear in prose and in verse, and it is difficult to know which is older. The Buddha did not speak in verse, but this may represent early attempts at remembering his teachings in what has been called 'the prism of memorialising verse'. These include some of the oldest doctrines and show something of the ancient Dharma. There is also a great deal of prose dialogue and narrative, much of it repetitive and sometimes tedious, and selection has to be made of what appear to be major interests of Buddhism. These selections are taken chiefly from the central collection of Buddhist dialogues according to southern Buddhism.

Theravada Buddhism came to be called Hina-yana, the 'lesser vehicle' of salvation, by rivals who claimed to have a more universal appeal. The Theravada reject this claim, along with the title Hinayana, since they assert that they have the original teachings. Today they are the Buddhists of Sri Lanka, Burma, Thailand, Cambodia and Laos. The

Maha-yana, 'great vehicle', developed ideas of other Buddhas and Buddhas-to-be, of Buddha-fields and a Western Paradise, absorbing much of the popular religion of China, Tibet, Korea and Japan.

Southern Buddhism holds that it is nearer to the teachings of the Buddha himself than the Mahayana, but it is not simply moral or ascetic teaching. The religion is expressed in beautiful pagodas and dagobas, in images and paintings, in rituals and pilgrimages to holy places. The monks retain their lead though in some places they have suffered in political and social turmoil, notably in Cambodia, and orders of nuns have disappeared.

These teachings of the Buddha and early Buddhists have been of great influence, though selections have always been made out of their great length. But it is a fallacy that religious books necessarily make easy reading, for many of them are obscure or complex. The Hindu Upanishads wryly remark that 'the gods love the cryptic and dislike the obvious'. The early Buddhists were sometimes cryptic and often very wordy, so that many abridgements have to be made to bring them within the scope of the general reader, especially those from different cultures.

The canonical scriptures of Theravada Buddhism are in the Pali language, and the whole has been gradually translated into English by the Pali Text Society during the last hundred years. The earlier volumes of this series in particular are in graceful English and have been used extensively here. Selections from these dialogues, arranged according to subject, may appeal to a wider public than would study the very extensive scriptures. Graceful language, humane spirit, religious devotion and moral endeavour appear as characteristic of Theravada Buddhism.

References

There have been several anthologies of Buddhist texts, from H.C. Warren, *Buddhism in Translations* (1896), to T. Ling, *The Buddha's Philosophy of Man* (1981). The first part of the Theravada Buddhist scriptures in the Pali language is the Vinaya or Discipline for monks, translated into English as Vinaya Texts from 1881. The next and major section is the Sutta, collection of verses, in which come the Digha, Long collection, English translation as *Dialogues of the Buddha* from 1899; Majjhima or Middle Length Sayings, in English from 1926; Samyutta, Kindred Sayings, in English 1917; Anguttara, Gradual Sayings, in English 1932. Shorter collections are Udana, Solemn Utterances, in English in 1902, and Sutta Nipata, Discourse collection, translated from 1874. The short and popular Dhammapada, Doctrine Path, has had various translations from 1881. The Lalita Vistara, Account of legends of the Buddha, and the Mahavastu, Great Story, are both in Sanskrit but from Theravada schools. The Questions of Milinda, about 100 BC in Pali, in English from 1880, gives discussions between a Greek King Menander and a Buddhist monk Nagasena, and although outside the canon of scripture it is authoritative and elucidates some basic teachings of the Buddha.

Family and Renunciation

The Buddha was staying at a cottage in a wood and he overheard his disciples discussing births.

He said: In this fortunate eon the Exalted One has now arisen in the world as a Supreme Buddha. He is of noble birth, born in a clan of nobles, in a family with the surname of Gautama. His chief attendant is Ananda, and two chief disciples Sariputta and Moggallana, a glorious pair. His father is the rajah Suddhodana, whose wife Maya is his mother, and their seat is the town of Kapilavastu. His leaving the world, becoming a recluse, his travail, his enlightenment, his setting the Wheel of Truth rolling, are each on such and such wise.

Digha 2,1,51-2

I myself before my enlightenment, while unenlightened and yet a bodhisattva [being of enlightenment], being myself liable to rebirth, sought out what was liable to rebirth: in old age, sickness, death, grief and depravity. Then this occurred to me: Why should I, who am liable to rebirth, seek out what is liable to rebirth, in these things? What if I, seeing the wretchedness of what is liable to rebirth, were to seek for the unborn, the supreme peace of Nirvana?

Majjhima 1,160

There are two searches, the noble and the ignoble. In the ignoble search a person though himself liable to rebirth seeks out what is liable to old age, to sickness, to death, to grief, and to depravity. All objects of attachment are liable to rebirth, and to these objects a person is tied, with them he is infatuated, and to them he is attached.

In the noble search a person sees the wretchedness of rebirth, and seeks for the unborn, the supreme peace, Nirvana.

ibid.

So while I was yet a youth, black-haired and in my prime, in the first years of manhood, against the wishes of my mother and my father who lamented me with tear-stained faces, I had the hair of my head and face shaved off. I put on saffron robes and went forth from my Home to the Homeless life. I became a wanderer and a searcher for what is good, what cannot be surpassed, and I sought the supreme state of peace.

ibid.

At twenty-nine I sought the Good
and worldly luxuries forswore.
And then a pilgrim's path pursued
for fifty years and one year more,
where one alone can victory win
thro' Doctrine and thro' discipline.

Digha 2,151

The Four Signs

The Buddha-to-be bade his charioteer get ready his carriage to drive through the park. There he saw an old man, bent as a roof gable, tottering and leaning on a staff. He asked his charioteer:

That man, what has he done, that his hair and body are not like those of other men?

He is what is called an old man, my lord, because he has not long to live.

But then am I too subject to old age?

Yes, my lord, we are all of a kind to grow old.

Then enough of the park for today, drive me back.

He returned to his rooms sorrowful and depressed, thinking, Shame be upon this thing called birth, since old age shows itself like that.

Digha 2,21

After a time the Buddha-to-be driving to the park saw a sick man, suffering, fallen to the ground, being lifted by others and dressed by them. He asked his charioteer:

That man, what has he done, that his eyes are not like other men's, nor his voice like other men's?

He is what is called ill, my lord, he will hardly recover.

But then am I too subject to illness?

Yes, my lord, we are all of a kind to fall ill.

Then enough of the park for today, drive me back.

He returned to his rooms sorrowful and depressed, thinking, Shame be upon this thing called birth, since to one born decay and disease show themselves like that.

ibid. 2,24

After a time the Buddha-to-be driving to the park saw a great crowd of people in garments of different colours, making a funeral pyre. He asked his charioteer:

Why are those people making that pile of wood?

It is because someone, my lord, has ended his days.

What is the meaning of ending one's days?

It means that neither mother nor father, nor other kinsfolk, will see him any more, nor will he ever again see them.

But then am I too subject to death? Will neither the rajah, nor the ranee, nor any of my kind see me more, nor I ever again see them?

Yes, my lord, we are all subject to death.

Then enough of the park for today, drive me back.

He returned to his rooms sorrowful and depressed, thinking, Shame be upon this thing called birth, since decay of life, disease, and death show like that.

ibid. 2,25

After a time, the Buddha-to-be driving to the park saw a shaven-headed man, a Wanderer, wearing a yellow robe. He asked his charioteer:

What has that man done, that his head is unlike those of other men and his clothes different from theirs?

That is what they call a Wanderer, my lord, one who has gone forth.

What is that, to have gone forth?

It means to be thorough in the religious life, my lord, thorough in peaceful life, in good actions, in meritorious conduct, in harmlessness, in kindness to all creatures.

The Buddha-to-be said: Excellent indeed, O charioteer, is what they call a Wanderer. You take the carriage back to my palace. I will now cut off my hair, don the yellow robe, and go forth from Home into the Homeless state.

ibid. 2,28

Search and Enlightenment

The Buddha said: When I went forth from the world I sought the good and the highest state of peace. I approached the ascetic Alara and asked to practise his religious discipline. I mastered it in no long time and found he proclaimed the attainment of a state of Nothingness. Then I thought, this doctrine does not lead to absence of passion, cessation, tranquillity, higher knowledge and Nirvana. So I abandoned this doctrine in disgust.

Majjhima 1,160

Then I approached another teacher, Uddaka, and asked to practise the religious life in his doctrine and discipline. But he taught the attainment of Neither-consciousness-nor-non-consciousness. I found that this doctrine does not lead to absence of passion, cessation, tranquillity, higher knowledge and Nirvana. So I abandoned this doctrine in disgust.

ibid.

Ever seeking to attain the calm of peace, I came to a woodland grove, with a clear flowing river, and a village nearby for support. Here the tempter Mara came to me, urging that life is better than non-life, death is near, and the body should not be wearied. To him I answered that life ends in death, lusts are his army, with craving, sloth, hunger, fear, doubt, anger and hypocrisy. With my wisdom I crushed that army of his, and wandered on fully conscious.

Lalita-vistara 327

Then I set to practise austerities. I restrained breathing in and out, and I practised trance without breathing. I took food only in small amounts, and thought to refrain from food altogether. My body became extremely lean, my ribs stuck out like the beams of an old shed, and when I thought I would touch the skin of my stomach I actually took hold of my spine. Five other ascetics came to watch me, thinking that when I attained to the truth I would tell it to them. But I came to think that by such severe mortification I do not attain true knowledge and insight, perhaps there is a Middle Way which cannot be followed when the body is weak. I got up and took some rice-milk from the daughter of the village headman and ate some beans, but the five ascetics left me in disgust.

Majjhima 1,242

When I had taken food I sat under the shade of a tree, free from sensual desires and evil thoughts. I entered the first state of meditation arising from seclusion and reasoning. Next I entered the second state beyond reasoning. Then the third state, attentive and conscious. Finally the fourth state, entirely pure and mindful. I remembered all my former existences, I saw all beings arising and passing away, I sought the unborn and undecaying and undying. In the last watch of the night I was released, and I knew that rebirth is destroyed, the religious life has been led, done is what was to be done, there is nothing further in this world.

ibid.

Then I thought, I have gained the Doctrine which is hard to perceive and to be known only by the wise. If I were to teach the Doctrine and others did not understand it, it would be a weariness and vexation to me, and as I reflected my mind turned to inaction.

Then the chief of the gods, Brahma, thought that the world would be destroyed if the Doctrine was not taught. He vanished from heaven and appeared before me, with robe over one shoulder and hands joined and said, Let the Lord teach the Doctrine. There are beings with but little dust in their eyes who will grow if they hear it. So I surveyed the world with my Buddha-vision, and I saw that as with blue, red or white lotuses some do not rise out of the water but others stand out unstained, so there are beings of little impurity or much impurity, of keen or dull faculties, and I declared to Brahma that the doors of No More Death are open for those who hear. ibid.

Then I considered who would learn the Doctrine quickly. I thought of Alara, but I was told he had passed away seven days before. I thought that Uddaka would understand quickly, and was told that he had passed away last night. Then I thought I would teach the Doctrine to the five ascetics, and by my purified vision I saw them dwelling in the Deer Park at Sarnath by Benares, so I made my way there. When the ascetics saw me coming they said, This is Gautama who has given up striving and lives in abundance, we must not greet him nor rise in respect nor take his bowl and robe. But as I approached they were not able to keep to their decision and they prepared a seat and set water for my feet. To them I said, I am a Buddha, fully enlightened, I have attained the immortal, give ear to my Doctrine. I taught them the Middle Way, avoiding the extremes of sensuality and self-torture, setting in motion the Wheel of Doctrine with the Four Noble Truths, the Noble Eightfold Path, and the Marks of Not-self.
Majjhima 1,167

O builder of the house, now you are seen. You will not build the house again. All your rafters are broken, your ridge-pole is destroyed. Your mind has attained the extinction of desires. It is set on the attainment of Nirvana.
Dhammapada 154

The Four Noble Truths

This is the noble truth of pain: birth is painful; old age, sickness, death, sorrow, despair are painful.
 This is the noble truth of the cause of pain: it is craving, which leads to rebirth, combined with pleasure and lust,

craving for existence and non-existence.

This is the noble truth of the cessation of pain: cessation without remainder of that craving; forsaking, non-attachment.

This is the noble truth of the way that leads to the cessation of pain: it is the Noble Eightfold Path.

Samyutta 5,420

One who takes refuge in the Buddha, the Doctrine, and the Order, perceives by clear wisdom the Four Noble Truths: suffering, the cause of suffering, the cessation of suffering, and the Noble Eightfold Path which brings cessation of suffering. Dhammapada 190-1

Now there are these four Noble truths.
What four?
They are the Noble Truth of ill, the Noble Truth of the origins of ill, the Noble Truth of the stopping of ill, the Noble Truth of the way that leads to the stopping of ill.
What is the Noble Truth of ill?
It is this: birth is ill, age is ill, disease is ill, death is ill, failure to get what one wants is ill; the body and the feelings and the perceptions and the impulses and the consciousness, in a word all the five components of grasping at material things are ill. Mahavastu 3,331

When my knowledge and insight was purified by these Four Noble Truths, then I had attained the highest complete enlightenment. Knowledge arose in me that the release of my mind is unshakeable: this is my last existence; now there is no rebirth. Samyutta 5,420

What have I declared?
The fact of pain, the cause of pain, the cessation of pain, the Way leading to the cessation of pain.
And why have I declared it?
Because it is profitable, it belongs to the beginning of the religious life, and tends to renunciation, absence of passion, calm, higher knowledge, enlightenment and Nirvana. Therefore I have declared it. ibid. 5,437

You must be devoted to this: this is pain, this is the cause of pain, this is the cessation of pain, this is the Way leading to the cessation of pain. ibid.

One who is enlightened knows the fact: These are the Deadly Floods [of illusion and defilement].

He knows: This is the origin of the Deadly Floods.

He knows: This is the cessation of the Deadly Floods.

He knows: This is the Path that leads to the cessation of the Deadly Floods.

To him who knows and sees this the heart is set free from the Deadly Taint of Lusts.

It is set free from the Deadly Taint of Becomings.

It is set free from the Deadly Taint of Ignorance.

Being set free there arises in him the knowledge of his freedom and he knows: Rebirth has been destroyed. The higher life has been fulfilled. What had to be done has been done. Now there is no rebirth.

Digha 1,84

The Noble Eightfold Path

This is the noble truth of the way that leads to the cessation of pain: it is the Noble Eightfold Path, namely: Right views, Right intention, Right speech, Right action, Right livelihood, Right effort, Right mindfulness, Right concentration.

This Noble Eightfold Path is to be practised.

Samyutta 5,420

What is the Noble [Aryan] Truth of the stopping of ill?

It is the Noble Eightfold Way, namely: Right belief, Right purpose, Right speech, Right action, Right living, Right endeavour, Right mindfulness, Right contemplation. This is the Noble Truth that leads to the stopping of ill.

From the truth 'This is the stopping of ill', by full attention to things unheard of before, there arose in me knowledge, vision, understanding, insight, wisdom and light. I realised unshakeable freedom of heart, through intuitive wisdom.

Mahavastu 3,333

The Noble Eightfold Path is itself the course leading to the stopping of Karma formations. One who has come into this true Doctrine, who sees this true Doctrine, who is endowed with the lore of a learner, who has reached the stream of Doctrine, he stands knocking at the door of the Deathless.

Samyutta 2,43

The Middle Way

At one time the Buddha dwelt in a Deer Park near Benares. There he addressed his five first disciples:

There are two extremes which are not to be practised. What are these two?

That which is joined to the passions and luxury, which is low, vulgar, common, ignoble and useless. And that which is joined to self-torture, which is painful, ignoble and useless. Avoiding the extremes of sensuality and self-torture, the knowledge of the Middle Way brings insight, calm, enlightenment and Nirvana.

What is the Middle Way, by which the Buddha has gained enlightenment, and which produces insight and knowledge, and which tends to calm, to the higher knowledge and enlightenment and Nirvana?

It is the Noble Eightfold Way. This is the Middle Path.

Samyutta 5,420

Of all paths the Eightfold is the best.

This is the path; there is no other that leads to purification of insight.

Follow this path, that will be to escape from evil.

Going on this path you will end suffering.

I preached this path when I knew how to remove the thorns of grief.

Those who enter the path, and practise meditation, are released from the bonds of evil.

'All created things are transitory.' When one realises this

he is superior to sorrow. This is the path of purity.

'All created things are sorrowful.' When one realises this he is superior to sorrow. This is the path of purity.

Cut out the love of self, as you would cut an autumn lily by hand. Cherish the path to peace, to Nirvana.

Dhammapada 273-285

As the waters of the Ganges and the Jumna flow into one another and go on together united, so it is with the well-revealed Way which leads to Nirvana. They run one into the other, the Way and Nirvana. Only the Exalted One, the Buddha, is a revealer of this kind, of such a Way leading to Nirvana, whether we survey the past or the present.

Digha 2,223

The Lord was the producer of the unproduced Way, the originator of the unoriginated Way, the preacher of the unpreached Way, the knower, understander, and perceiver of the Way.

Majjhima 3,7

The Marks of Not-Self

The body is not the self [soul].

If the body were the self, it would not be subject to sickness.

The feelings are not the self.
Perceptions are not the self.
Impulses are not the self.
Consciousness is not the self.

Samyutta 3,66

If one does not discern any self, or anything like a self, in the five groups of shape, feeling, perception, impulses and consciousness, one is learned, with defilements extinguished.

ibid. 3,127

Material shape and the other elements are impermanent, what is impermanent is ill, what is ill is not-self. What is not-self – this is not mine, I am not this, this is not my self.
Vinaya 1,14

A speculative view holds: that self of mine is permanent, stable, and eternal, it will remain like the eternal. This speculative view is wild, wriggling, scuffling, and a chain.
Majjhima 1,8

When ignorance has been put away, and knowledge has grown, there is no grasping after the pleasures of sense, or after speculations, or after rituals, or after the theory of self.
ibid. 1,67

The instructed disciple considers of the material shape, and the other elements: 'This is not mine, I am not this, this is not my self.' So that when these elements change and become different he has no grief, or sorrow, or suffering, or lamentation, or despair.
Samyutta 3,19

A certain disciple said to the Buddha, Can there be freedom from worry about what does not exist outwardly?
The Buddha replied, There can. An understanding disciple does not think: Alas, it was not mine, or might be mine. He does not grieve, or lament, or beat his breast, or become bewildered. He has freedom from worry about what does not exist outwardly.
Majjhima 1,135

Some ascetics and priests accuse me wrongly and groundlessly, saying that the Buddha is a nihilist, preaching the annihilation or non-existence of an existent being. I am not that and do not say that. Both previously and now I teach the truth of suffering, and the cessation of suffering.
ibid.

The self is lord of self. Who else could be its lord? If the self is well subdued one finds a lord who is difficult to grasp.
Dhammapada 160

King Milinda asked the monk Nagasena, What is your name?
He replied, I am known as Nagasena, but though my

parents gave me this name, it is just a practical designation, a mere name, for no real person can be apprehended here.

The king said, Now listen you Greeks, Nagasena tells me he is not a real person. How can I agree with that? For if no person can be apprehended in reality, who gives you food and lodging? Who is it that guards morality and practises meditation and realises the Four Noble Truths? If there was no person, there could be no reward or punishment, no fruit of good and evil. You would not be a real teacher or ordained monk. What is this Nagasena? Is it the hairs on your head, or parts of the body? Is it the feelings, or perceptions, or impulses, or consciousness? Or is it the combination of these things?

No, great king.

Then I discover no Nagasena at all. You have told a lie. There really is no Nagasena. Milinda 25

Nagasena replied, How did your Majesty come here?

He said, In a chariot.

What is a chariot? Is it the axle, wheels, frame, reins, yoke, spokes or goad?

It is none of these.

Are all these separate parts the chariot?

No.

Is there a chariot apart from them?

No.

Then I find no chariot at all. Your Majesty has spoken a lie. There really is no chariot.

The king said, It is in dependence on the parts that there comes this name chariot.

Nagasena said, Your Majesty has spoken well. It is in dependence on the parts of the body and the five elements that there takes place this designation Nagasena. But in ultimate reality, this person cannot be apprehended. So there is this verse which a nun recited to the Buddha:

When all the parts are rightly set
The word Chariot is applied;
And where the elements exist
The term a 'being' is applied.

ibid. 27

The Buddha

In the Shakya clan there was born a Buddha, peerless among men, conqueror of all, repeller of evil. He is all-seeing. He has won extinction of all karma, and is freed by removal of defilements.

Samyutta 1,134

I am not a priest, nor a rajah's son, nor a merchant, nor do I belong to any class. I fare forth in the world as a sage, without craving, homeless, with self completely gone out. It is foolish to ask of my lineage.

Sutta Nipata 455

I am the Victor over all,
Omniscient and pure,
From craving free, and leaving all,
Know by myself and point to none.

Majjhima 1,213

The outward form of him who has won the truth stands before you, but that which binds it to rebirth is cut in two. So long as his body lasts, so long will gods and men behold him. When the body is dissolved, after the end of his earthly life, neither gods nor men will see him.

Digha 1,46

What is there in seeing this vile body? Whoever sees the Doctrine sees me; he who sees me sees the Doctrine.

Samyutta 3,120

A priest asked the Buddha:
  Is your honour a god?
  He replied:
  No, indeed, I am not a god.
  Then a heavenly spirit?
  No, indeed.
  Then a demigod?

The Buddha [25]

No, indeed.
Then is your honour a human being?
No, I am not a human being.
You answer No to all my questions. What then are you?
The Buddha replied: All those defilements by which, if they had not been extinguished, I might have been a god, a heavenly spirit, a demigod or a human being, have been extinguished in me. Just as a blue, red or white lotus, although it has grown up in the water is unsoiled by water when it reaches the surface, so although I was born in the world I have overcome the world and I abide unsoiled in the world. Take it that I am Buddha, the Awakened One.
Anguttara 2,37

When I used to enter various large assemblies, even before I had sat down or had spoken, I used to become in colour like their colour, and in language like their language. I instructed and quickened them and filled them with gladness, with religious Doctrine, and they would say: Who is this that speaks thus? Is he a man or a god? And I would vanish away.
Digha 2,109

The Buddha is freed from material shape, feeling, perception, impulses and consciousness. Like the ocean, he is deep, immeasurable, and unfathomable. So you cannot apply to him that he arises, or does not arise, or both arises and does not arise, or neither arises or does not arise.
Majjhima 1,487

Since a Buddha is incomprehensible, even when actually present, it is foolish to say of him, who is the Uttermost Person, the Attainer of the Highest, that after dying the Buddha is, or is not, or both is and is not, or neither is nor is not.
Samyutta 3,118

The Buddha is a seer of what is to be seen, but he is unaffected by the seen, the unseen, the seeable, and the seer. So is he with the heard, the sensed, and the known, he is unaffected by these modes. He is precisely 'such'.
Anguttara 2,25

He whose faith in the Buddha is settled, rooted, established and firm, a faith not to be shaken by an ascetic or a priest or a god or a demon, or by anyone in the world, he may well say: I am a true son of the Lord, born from his mouth, born of the Doctrine, formed by the Doctrine, heir of the Doctrine. And why? Because these names are equivalent to Buddha: Doctrine-body, and again the Highest-body; and again Doctrine-become, and again the Highest-become.

Digha 3,84

There appears in the world one who has won the truth, a fully awakened one, abounding in wisdom and goodness, who knows all worlds, unsurpassed as a guide to mortals, a teacher for gods and men, a Blessed One, a Buddha.

He by himself thoroughly knows and sees this universe face to face, including the world above of the gods, and the world below with its priests and princes and peoples. Having known it, he makes his knowledge known to others. He proclaims the truth, lovely in its origin, its progress and its consummation, in spirit and in letter. He makes known the higher life in all its fullness and purity.

ibid. 1,62

It is impossible that in one world two Perfect Buddhas should arise simultaneously.

If a second Buddha were to arise the world-system could not sustain him; it would tremble, shake, bend, bow down, twist, disperse, scatter, disappear.

If two Perfect Buddhas were to arise at the same moment there would be dispute among their assemblies, saying: Your Buddha, our Buddha, and a two-fold faction might be brought into existence.

Other things that are mighty in the world are also unique. The earth is mighty and unique; the sea is mighty and unique; the chief of the gods is mighty and unique; and the Perfect Buddha is mighty and unique in the world.

Milinda 237-9

It may be that Wanderers teaching other doctrines than ours may say: Does a Buddha exist after death? Is that true and any other view absurd?

They are to be answered: This has not been revealed by the Buddha.

Or they may say: Does a Buddha not exist after death? Or does a Buddha neither exist nor not exist after death? Or

does he both exist and not exist after death?
They are to be answered in the same words.

Digha 3,135

There are thirty-two special marks of the Superman, and for the Superman possessing them two careers lie open, and none other. If he lives the life of the House, he becomes a Monarch, a Turner of the Wheel, a righteous Lord of the Right, Ruler of the four quarters, Conqueror, Guardian of the people's good.

But if such a boy goes forth from the life of the House to the Homeless state, he becomes a Supreme Buddha, rolling back the veil from the world.

ibid. 3,142

The Lord's City of Doctrine has virtue for its ramparts, the moats are conscience, the gates are knowledge, the turrets are energy, the pillars are faith, its watchmen are mindfulness, its palace is wisdom, its crossroads are the Discourses, the roads are the Supplementary Doctrines, the law court is the Discipline, its main street is earnest self-control.

Milinda 332

Does the Buddha still exist?

Yes, he does.

Then is it possible to point out the Buddha, as being here or there?

No, he cannot be pointed out as here or there. The Lord has attained final Nirvana, so that nothing is left which could lead to the formation of another being.

Give me an illustration.

If the flame of a great fire has gone out, is it possible to say that it is either here or there?

No, the flame has stopped, it has disappeared.

Even so, the Lord has passed away in Nirvana, with nothing left for future birth. The Lord has gone home, and it is not possible to point to him or say that he is here or there. But it is possible to point to the Lord in the body of his Doctrine, for the Doctrine was taught by the Lord.

ibid. 73

The Doctrine

The Doctrine is well taught by the Buddha, it is thoroughly seen here and now, it is timeless, inviting all to come and see, leading upwards, and to be understood by the wise each for himself. Majjhima 1,36

When one thinks that he has unwavering confidence in the Buddha, the Doctrine, and the Order, he acquires knowledge of the Doctrine and the delight connected with the Doctrine. Rapture is born from that delight, and so his body is immune to suffering, therefore joy is felt, and the mind is well concentrated. ibid.

If one teaches the Doctrine for the turning away from material shape, from feeling, perception, impulses and consciousness, for indifference to them, and for their cessation, it is fitting to call such a one a speaker of Doctrine, and one who has attained Nirvana here and now.
Samyutta 3,163

The Doctrine has been well declared by me, made manifest, disclosed, brought to light, stripped of bonds. It is enough for a wellbred young man who has abandoned all through faith to think, I would gladly be reduced to skin and bones, and let my flesh and blood dry up, if there came an access of vigour so that the goal might be won by human strength and vigour and striving. ibid. 2,28

As the lion, the king of beasts, is reckoned chief among animals, for his strength and speed and bravery, so is the faculty of wisdom reckoned chief among those mental states which are helpful for enlightenment.
ibid. 5,227

It is through not understanding this Doctrine, through not penetrating it, that this generation has become tangled like a ball of thread, covered with blight, twisted like a grass

The Doctrine

rope, unable to pass beyond the state of sorrow, the woeful way, the abyss, the constant round of transmigration.

Digha 2,55

The Buddha taught the Doctrine for passing beyond birth, for getting rid of all suffering; he established me in truth.

Samyutta 1,132

I will teach you Doctrine by the parable of the Raft.

A man going along a road might see a great stretch of water, but if there were no boat or a bridge for crossing it, he might think, If I were to collect wood and foliage and make a raft, I might cross over safely. If he carried out his purpose and crossed over, he might think again. This raft has been very useful to me, if I carried it on my head I could proceed as I desire. If a man did that would he do what should be done with the raft?

No, Lord, answered the disciples.

Then it might occur to him after he has crossed, This raft has been very useful to me, but I will beach it on dry ground, or submerge it in water, and then proceed as I desire. In doing this, he would do what should be done with the raft. Even so the Doctrine is for crossing over, not for retaining. You should get rid of unwholesome mental states, and even of wholesome ones.

Majjhima 1,134

Teach the Doctrine, that is lovely at the beginning, lovely in the middle, and lovely at the end. Explain with the spirit and the letter the Doctrine fulfilled and pure. There are beings with little dust in their eyes who, not hearing the Doctrine, are decaying. But if they learn the Doctrine they will grow.

Vinaya 1,20

There is no disappearing of the true Doctrine until a counterfeit doctrine appears in the world. It is when foolish persons arise that they make the true Doctrine disappear. But monks and nuns, laymen and laywomen, should live with reverence for the Buddha, the Doctrine and the Order, for training and for concentration.

Samyutta 2,224

I have taught the Doctrine without making any distinction between esoteric and exoteric, for the Buddha has no such thing as the closed fist of a teacher who keeps some things back in respect of the truth.

Digha 2,100

Just as the great ocean has one taste, the taste of salt, even so this Doctrine and discipline has one taste, the taste of release.
Vinaya 2,239

Live as islands to yourselves, as refuges to yourselves, taking no other refuge. Live with the Doctrine as your island, with the Doctrine as your refuge, taking no other refuge.
Digha 3,58

The Doctrine is best among all peoples,
In this life and the next.
ibid. 3,83

The Order

If outsiders should speak against the Buddha, or against the Doctrine, or against the Order, you should not bear malice or suffer heart-burning.

Likewise if outsiders should praise the Buddha, or praise the Doctrine, or praise the Order, you should not be filled with pleasure or be lifted up in heart. Were you to be so that would stand in the way of your self-conquest.
Digha 1,3

A synonym for the disciple is: the priest who crossed over, went beyond, stands on dry land.
Samyutta 4,175

He whose passions are extinguished, who is indifferent to food, who has perceived the nature of release and freedom, his path is as difficult to understand as that of birds in the sky.
Dhammapada 93

You have not a mother or a father who might care for you, O monks. If you do not care for each other, who will care for you? Whosoever would care for me, he should care for the sick.
Vinaya 1,302

The Order

Walk on tour for the blessing of many, for the happiness of many, out of compassion for the world, for the welfare and the blessing and the happiness of gods and men.

ibid. 1,20

One should not knowingly make use of meat killed on purpose for one. Whoever should make use of it offends by wrong-doing. Fish and meat are allowed as pure in three respects: if they have not been seen, or heard, or suspected, to have been killed on purpose for you.

ibid. 1,236

The household life is full of hindrances, it is a path for the dust of passion. The life of him who has renounced worldly things is free as the air. How difficult is it for the man who dwells at home to live the higher life in all its fullness and purity and perfection. So let me cut off my hair and beard, clothe myself in saffron-coloured robes, and go forth from Home to the Homeless state.

Digha 1,62

A village headman asked: Is the Lord compassionate towards all living creatures?.
Yes, replied the Buddha.
The man asked, But does the Lord teach the Doctrine in full to some but not so to others?
The Buddha replied, Suppose a farmer had three fields; one excellent, one mediocre, and one with bad soil. Which field would he sow first? He would sow the excellent one, then the mediocre one. Then he might or might not sow the poor one, because it might do for cattle-fodder.
In the same way, my monks and nuns are the excellent field, to whom I teach the Doctrine in its fullness. Then my men and women lay followers are the mediocre field, to whom also I teach the Doctrine, and who come to me for refuge. Then priests and wanderers of other sects are like the poor field. When I teach the Doctrine to them, if they understood even a single sentence that would give them happiness for a long time.

Samyutta 4,314

The Buddha's cousin Devadatta sought to enrich himself, and take command of the Order.
He said, You, Lord, are now old and near the close of life. Be content to abide in ease here. It is I who will lead the Order of monks.

The Sayings of the Buddha

The Buddha said, I would not hand over the Order even to my chief disciples Sariputta and Moggallana, how much less to a wretch like you. Let the Order of monks see that Devadatta's nature has changed. Whatever he does neither the Buddha nor the Doctrine nor the Order are to be seen, but only Devadatta. Devadatta got a fierce elephant to rush at the Buddha, but the Lord calmed it with loving-kindness, stroked his trunk with his right hand and spoke some verses. The elephant took the dust of the Lord's feet and scattered it over his head, bowing while he gazed on the Lord and then returned to his stable.

Then the Buddha said, Do not let there be a schism in the Order. He that splits an Order sets up defilement that endures for an eon and he is boiled in hell for an eon. But he who unites an Order that is split gains merit and rejoices in heaven for an eon.   Vinaya 2,184

I will teach you seven conditions for the welfare of a community:

so long as the brothers foregather often and frequent the formal meetings of the Order;

so long as they meet together in concord and carry out the duties of the Order in concord;

so long as the brothers shall establish nothing that has not been already prescribed, and act in accordance with the rules;

so long as the brothers honour and support the elders of experience and hearken to their words;

so long as they delight in a life of solitude;

so long as they train their minds in self-possession so that good men may come to them;

so long may the brothers be expected not to decline but to prosper.   Digha 2,77

How is a disciple accomplished in morality?
He refrains from taking life.
He abstains from taking what is not given.
He abandons unchastity.
He abstains from falsehood.
He abstains from intoxicants.
He eats only within one meal time.
He refrains from seeing dancing, singing and music.
He refrains from scents and garlands, from a high or

large bed, from accepting gold and silver.

He refrains from accepting women, slaves, animals and lands.

He refrains from buying and selling, from cheating and fraud, from killing and violence.

[the first five of these rules are also for lay people]

ibid. 1,47ff

Women, Nuns

The chief disciple Ananda asked, How are we to conduct ourselves with regard to women?

The Buddha replied, As not seeing them.

He asked, But if we should see them, what are we to do?

No talking, Ananda.

But if they should speak to us, what are we to do?

Keep wide awake, Ananda.

Digha 2,141

The Buddha's aunt, Pajapati, asked, May women leave home for the homeless state, in the Doctrine and Discipline proclaimed by the Buddha?

The Buddha replied, Be careful of the going forth of women from home to the homeless state.

This was done three times, and Pajapati was grieved and crying. She cut off her hair, donned saffron robes, and stood outside weeping, covered with dust and with swollen limbs. There Ananda saw her, and told her to wait while he asked the Lord about women going to the homeless state. But the Buddha answered as he had Pajapati, so Ananda put a different question:

Suppose women have left home in this Doctrine and Discipline, can they win the fruits of enlightenment and discipleship?

Yes, Ananda, replied the Buddha. If they accept the rules of the Order, do homage to ordained monks, do not reside on their own, are trained for two years, and seek ordination from the Orders of monks and nuns. If they honour and respect and revere and venerate the rules, then I allow nuns to be ordained by monks. *Vinaya 2,253*

A laywoman supporter said, Lord, I want to give clothes for the Order for life during the rains, food for those coming in and out, food for the sick and those who nurse them, a constant supply of rice-milk, and bathing-clothes for nuns.

She continued, There was a case where nuns bathed naked together with prostitutes at a river ford, and the prostitutes made fun of them, saying; Why on earth are you nuns while you are still young? Surely sense-pleasures should be enjoyed? When you are old you can become nuns, and so you will experience both extremes. The nuns were ashamed. Nakedness is impure for women, it is abhorrent and objectionable. For this special reason I want to give bathing-clothes for nuns for life.

The Buddha replied, It is very good that you have said this and I accept it. *ibid. 1,294*

A courtesan heard that the Exalted One was staying in her mango grove, and she went on foot to where he was and took her seat respectfully on one side. And when she was thus seated the Exalted One instructed, aroused, incited and gladdened her with religious discourse.

Then she said, May the Exalted One do me the honour of taking his meal at my house tomorrow, together with the brethren. And the Exalted One gave his consent by silence.

On the morrow she set food before the Order, with the Buddha at their head, and waited upon them till they refused any more. Then she said, I present this place to the Order of which the Buddha is the chief.

And the Exalted One accepted the gift, and after instructing, and rousing, and inciting, and gladdening her with religious discourse, he rose from his seat and departed. *Digha 2,95-8*

If women had not received the going forth from Home to a Homeless life, in the Doctrine and discipline declared by the Buddha, the good Doctrine would remain for a thousand years. But as women have gone forth now the religious life will not last long, now the good Doctrine will only last five hundred years. Just as houses where there are many women and few men are broken into by robbers, even so in that Doctrine and discipline in which women receive the going forth from Home to a Homeless life, the religious life will not last long.   Vinaya 10,1

There was a nun called Soma who dressed herself in the morning, took her bowl and robe, and went on her begging round. When she returned, after her meal, she went into a wood to stay in the open air.

Then the tempter Mara, wishing to produce fear and hair-raising in Soma and make her fall from her state of contemplation, drew near and said to her, The goal is hard to reach, hard even for sages; it cannot be won by a woman with whatever wisdom she may have.

Then Soma thought, Is it a man or a superhuman being who is saying this? It is the wicked Mara who wants to produce fear and hair-raising in me and make me fall from my state of contemplation. So seeing that it was Mara she said to him, What does the woman's state matter to one whose mind is well-composed, in whom knowledge is arising, and who contemplates the true Doctrine? Should there be anyone who thinks that I am a woman or a man or again something else, let Mara deign to speak to him.

The wicked Mara thought, The nun Soma knows me. So being pained and sad he thereupon disappeared.

Samyutta 1,129

Lay Followers

In the noble disciple four vices of action are put away, and he does not follow six things that lead to loss of wealth. What are his four vices of action that are dispelled?

Taking life, stealing, wrong indulgence in the passions, and falsehood.

What six things lead to loss of wealth?

Addiction to carelessness in strong drink, to frequenting

the streets at untimely hours, visiting feasts, carelessness in gambling, bad friends, and laziness.
Digha 3,181

A noble lay disciple reflects: Throughout life the monks shun and abandon taking life. I will imitate the monks and keep the Fast-day. I too today, for this night and day, shun and abandon taking life. I too today shun and abandon taking what is not given. I too today shun and abandon incontinence. I too today shun and abandon falsehood. I too today shun and abandon strong drink.
Anguttara 4,248

There are five misfortunes of an immoral person:
    a person who is immoral incurs great loss of wealth;
    evil fame is spread abroad about him;
    whatever assembly he enters he is confused;
    he dies with his mind in confusion;
    after death he is reborn in a state of misery, in an unhappy destiny, in a state of punishment, or in hell.
Digha 2,84

Reverence and gentleness, contentment and gratitude, hearing the Doctrine at due times; that is a supreme blessing.
    Insight into the Noble Truths, and the realisation of Nirvana, that is a supreme blessing.
Sutta-Nipata 2,4

Seven things tend to the benefit of a layman:
    he does not neglect seeing the monks;
    he is not careless about hearing the true Doctrine;
    he learns higher morality;
    he is well-disposed to all in the Order;
    he listens to the Doctrine without hostile mind, not looking for faults;
    he does not bestow gifts outside the Order;
    he gives his favours here.
Anguttara 4,25

Social Classes

There are these four classes: nobles, priests, merchants, and servants. Digha 1,91

The priests declare he is a true priest who has five things:
 he is of pure descent on both sides;
 he recites the scriptures;
 he is handsome and well formed, fair in colour;
 he is virtuous;
 he is learned and wise.
 Of these five things is it possible to leave one out and declare the man who has the other four to be a true priest?
 Yes, it can be done, we can leave out colour.
 Of these four can we leave one out?
 Yes, we can leave out recitation of scriptures. And so on, down to uprightness and wisdom.
 But what is that uprightness and wisdom?
 It is the Noble Eightfold Path, leading to full knowledge and concentration. ibid. 1,119

Seeing that both bad and good qualities are distributed among each of the four classes, the wise do not admit the claims which the priests put forward. Whoever among these classes becomes a monk, a worthy one, who has lived the life and done what had to be done and become free; he is declared chief among them because of the Doctrine.
 ibid. 3,83

What is the use of matted hair, or tattered goat-skins? You make the outside clean but the inner nature is evil. I do not call him a priest because of his father or mother. I call him a priest who has cut all fetters, who has passed beyond attachment and is enlightened.

I call him a priest who, like water on a lotus leaf or like a mustard seed on the point of an awl, does not cling to pleasures.

I call him a priest who is stainless like the moon, pure,

serene and undisturbed and in whom desires are extinguished.

I call him a priest whose wisdom is deep, who is without hostility, who utters true speech, who is free from impurity, who is fearless, noble and heroic.

Dhammapada 394-422

Even when a noble has fallen into the deepest degradation, still it holds good that the nobles are higher and the priests inferior.

It was one of the gods who uttered this verse:

The ruler is best among those men
Who trust in lineage.
The fully wise and righteous
Is best of all of gods and men.

Digha 1,99

I call him a priest who keeps away from both householders and mendicants, who does not frequent their houses, and has few wants.

Dhammapada 404

A householder said: I am old, advanced in years, ill in body and constantly ailing. Please instruct me for my welfare and happiness.

The Buddha said: You should train yourself to think, Though I am ill in body my mind shall not be ill. An unlearned common person, untrained in the Doctrine, is possessed by the thought, I am body, body is mine. A learned disciple, well-trained in the Doctrine, does not look upon feelings, or perceptions, or impulses, or consciousness as his self. His thought changes, and pain, dejection and despair do not arise. Even so, householder, one may be ill in body, but not in mind.

Samyutta 3,2

Social Duties

A son should minister to his parents in five ways:
Having been supported by them, I will now support them;
I will do my duty to them;
I will keep up the lineage and tradition of my family;
I will make myself worthy of my heritage;
I will provide an offering for their departed spirits.

Parents show their love to their child in five ways:
they restrain him from vice;
they exhort him to virtue;
they train him for a profession;
they find him a suitable wife;
in due time they hand over his inheritance.

Digha 3,189

A husband should minister to his wife in five ways:
by honouring her;
by respect;
by faithfulness;
by handing over authority to her;
by giving her ornaments;

A wife should love her husband in five ways:
by duties well performed;
by hospitality to relatives of both;
by faithfulness;
by looking after the stores;
by skill and industry in all her duties.

ibid. 3,190

A clansman should minister to his friends in five ways:
by generosity;
by courtesy;
by benevolence;
by treating them as he treats himself;
by being as good as his word.

His friends love him in five ways:
> they protect him when he is off his guard;
> on such occasions they guard his property;
> they become a refuge in danger;
> they do not forsake him in trouble;
> they show consideration for his family.

ibid.

A master should minister to his servants in five ways:
> by giving them work according to their strength;
> by supplying them food and wages;
> by tending them in sickness;
> by sharing special dainties with them;
> by giving them rest and holidays at proper times.

Servants and employees love their master in five ways:
> they rise before him;
> they go to bed after him;
> they do not steal;
> they do their work well;
> they give him a good report.

ibid. 3,191

He abused me, he struck me, he overcame me, he robbed me – In those who harbour such thoughts hatred will never cease. Enmities are not appeased at any time through enmity, but they are appeased through non-enmity. This is the eternal Doctrine.

Dhammapada 3-5

One who curbs his rising anger like a controlled chariot, him I call a real charioteer, others only hold the reins. Overcome evil with gentleness, overcome evil with good, overcome the miser with liberality, overcome lies with truth.

ibid. 222-223

Develop the state of mind of friendliness, for as you do this ill-will grows less. Develop compassion and anger grows less, develop joy and aversion grows less, develop equanimity and dislike grows less.

Majjhima 2,91

Karma

Beings have their own Karma. They are heirs of Karma, their origin is Karma, Karma is their kinsman, it is their resource. Karma distributes beings according to lowness and greatness.

A man or woman who takes life, killing with bloodstained hands and without mercy to living things, when his Karma is worked out, with the dissolution of the body after death, he is reborn in a state of misery, in an unhappy destiny, or in hell.

A man or woman who refrains from taking life, who is full of kindness and compassionate to all living things, when that Karma is worked out, with the dissolution of the body after death, he is reborn in a state of happiness, or is long lived, or is reborn in heaven.

Majjhima 3,202

There are four kinds of Karma. There is black Karma with black ripening; white Karma with white ripening; black and white Karma with black and white ripening; and Karma that is neither black nor white with neither black nor white ripening and which tends to the destruction of Karma.

ibid. 1,389

Why are men not all alike, but some are short-lived and some long, some sickly and some healthy, some ugly and some handsome, some weak and some strong, some poor and some rich, some base and some noble, some stupid and some clever?

It is because of different Karmas that all are not the same, but some are short-lived and some long, and so on. As the Lord said: Beings have their own Karma, they are born through Karma, they become members of tribes and families through Karma, they are all ruled by Karma, and it is Karma that divides them into high and low.

Milinda 65

That action is not well done which brings remorse, and whose result one receives with a tearful face. But that action is well done which does not bring remorse, and whose result one receives with delight.

Dhammapada 57-8

He whose evil action is covered by good actions, he lights up the world like the moon when it is freed from a cloud.

ibid. 173

This body is not yours, nor does it belong to others. It should be regarded as the product of former Karmas, brought about by what has been willed and felt. The wise one reflects on Conditioned Genesis: If this is, that comes to be; from the arising of this, that arises.

Samyutta 2,64

The Karma-formations are conditioned by ignorance. From the stopping of ignorance is the stopping of the Karma-formations.

Vinaya 1,1

From the arising of ignorance is the arising of the Karma-formations. The Noble Eightfold Path is the course leading to the stopping of the Karma-formations.

Samyutta 2,43

There are five blessings of a moral person through his morality:
    on account of his vigilance he acquires great wealth;
    good fame is spread abroad about him;
    when he enters an assembly he is confident and not confused;
    he dies without his mind being confused;
    with the dissolution of the body at death he is reborn in a state of happiness or in the world of heaven.

Digha 2,86

When consciousness has no resting-place, does not increase, and no longer accumulates Karma, it becomes free. When it is free it becomes quiet, blissful, not agitated, and it attains Nirvana in its own person. It knows that rebirth is exhausted, it has lived the holy life, it has done what had to be done, and that it is no more for this world.

Samyutta 22,53

Rebirth

To be born here and to die here, to die here and to be born elsewhere, to be born there and to die there, to die there and to be born elsewhere – that is the round of existence.
Milinda 77

I have circled through countless births seeking the builder of this house and have not found him; this birth is painful again and again.
Dhammapada 153

The beings born again among men are few. More numerous are those born elsewhere than among men.
Anguttara 1,35

The being is bound to transmigration; Karma is his means for going beyond.
Samyutta 1,38

Dying is for the born; he that is born sees the ills of bondage, misery and calamity. I take no pleasure in birth. The Buddha taught the Doctrine for passing beyond birth and getting rid of all suffering.
ibid. 1,132

When a man is born does he remain the same being or become another?
 He neither remains the same nor becomes another.
 Give me an example.
 You were once a baby lying on your back, tender and small and weak. Was that baby you, who are now grown up?
 No, the baby was one being and I am another.
 In that case you had no father or mother, and no teachers in learning, manners or wisdom.
Milinda 40

Suppose a man were to light a lamp, would it burn all the night through?
 Yes, it might.
 Now is the flame which burns in the middle watch the

same as that which burned in the first?
No.
Or is that which burns in the last watch the same as that which burned in the middle?
No.
So is there one lamp in the first watch, another in the middle, and yet another in the last?
No, the same lamp gives light all through the night.
Similarly the continuity of phenomena is kept up. One person comes into existence, another passes away, and the sequence runs continuously without self-conscious existence, neither the same nor yet another. ibid. 40

Is it true that nothing transmigrates, and yet there is rebirth?
Yes.
How can this be? Give me an illustration.
Suppose a man lights one lamp from another, does one lamp transmigrate to the other?
No.
So there is rebirth without anything transmigrating.
ibid. 71

It is because of the deeds one does, whether lovely or unlovely, by means of this name-and-shape [body], that one is linked again with another name-and-shape, and therefore one is not utterly freed from one's evil deeds.
ibid. 72

In beings subject to birth the wish arises: Ah, if only we were not subject to birth, if only we could avoid being born! But this is not to be got by wishing. This is the ill of not getting what is wished for. This is the Noble Truth regarding Ill. Digha 2,307

A brother by the complete destruction of the Three Bonds, of lust, illwill, and dullness, becomes a Once-returner, one who on his first return to this world shall make an end of pain. Further, a brother by the complete destruction of the Five Bonds, the above three with Sensuality and Doubt, that bind people to this world, becomes an inheritor of the highest heavens, there to pass away and never to return.
ibid. 1,156

It is through not understanding and grasping four truths, that we have had to wander so long in this weary path of transmigration, both you and I.

What are these four truths?

Noble conduct of life, earnestness in meditation, noble kind of wisdom, salvation of freedom. When these are realised and known, then the craving for future life is rooted out, that which leads to renewed existence is destroyed, and there is no more birth.
ibid. 2,122

The Buddha said: As far back as I wish I remember various previous births. As far as I wish with my divine purified vision surpassing human vision I see beings passing away and being reborn, low and exalted, fair and ugly, with happy or unhappy destinies.
Majjhima 1,482

That body, or feelings, or perceptions, or impulses, or consciousness, by which one might denote a released person, have passed away. They are cut down at the root, like a cutdown palm tree, made non-existent, not liable to arise again in the future. To say that one is reborn does not fit the case. To say that one is not reborn, or reborn and not reborn, or neither reborn or not reborn, does not fit the case.
ibid. 1,483

Nirvana

Nirvana is the stopping of becoming.
Samyutta 2,117

It is called Nirvana because of getting rid of craving.
ibid. 1,39

Conduct worthy of a holy one is lived for the plunge into Nirvana, for going beyond to Nirvana, for fulfilment in Nirvana.
ibid. 3,189

One who has wisdom here, who is devoid of desire and passions, attains to deathlessness, to peace, and to the unchanging state of Nirvana. Sutta Nipata 204

Where there is no-thing, where nothing is grasped, this is the island of No-beyond, I call it Nirvana. The utter extinction of ageing and dying. ibid. 1094

When he who was free from all craving
Who had reached the tranquil state of Nirvana,
When the great sage finished his span of life,
No gasping struggle vexed his steadfast heart.

Digha 2,157

It is said, Nirvana, Nirvana. Now what is Nirvana?
Whatever is the extinction of passion, and aversion, and confusion, this is Nirvana.
Is there a way for the realisation of this Nirvana?
There is. It is the Noble Eightfold Path, which itself is for the realisation of Nirvana. Samyutta 4,251

This is the real, this is the excellent, namely the extinction of all impulses, clinging, craving, and coming to dispassion, stopping, Nirvana. Anguttara 5,322

There is an unborn, not become, not made, uncompounded, and were it not for this unborn, not become, not made, uncompounded, there could be shown here no escape for what is born, has become, is made, and is compounded. Udana 80

Health is the greatest gift, contentment is the greatest wealth, trust is the best relationship. Nirvana is the highest happiness. Dhammapada 204

As a lotus is unsoiled by water, so is Nirvana unsoiled by any defilement.
As water that is cool is the means of allaying fever, so is Nirvana, which is cool, the means of allaying the fever of all defilements. Milinda 318

As a mountain-peak is lofty, so is Nirvana.
As a mountain-peak is immovable, so is Nirvana.

As a mountain-peak is hard to scale, so is Nirvana.
As no seeds can take root on a mountain-peak, so no defilements can take root in Nirvana.
As a mountain-peak is free from all desire to please or displease, so is Nirvana. ibid. 322

What is Nirvana like?
Is there something called wind?
Yes.
Please show me the wind by its colour, or shape, or whether it is thin or thick, long or short.
Even so, Nirvana exists, though it is not possible to point out Nirvana either by colour or shape. ibid. 270

Meditation

He chooses some lonely spot to rest at. He seats himself, when his meal is done, cross-legged, keeping his body erect, and his intelligence alert, intent.

Putting away the hankering after the world, he purifies his mind of lusts. Putting away the corruption of the wish to injure, he purifies his mind of malevolence. Putting away torpor of heart and mind, mindful and self-possessed, he purifies his mind of weakness and sloth. Putting away flurry and worry, with heart serene, he purifies himself of irritability and vexation of spirit. Putting away wavering, he remains as one who has passed beyond perplexity. No longer in suspense as to what is good, he purifies his mind of doubt. Digha 1,71

Putting away all hindrances, he lets his mind full of love pervade one quarter of the world, and so too the second quarter, and so the third, and so the fourth. And thus the whole wide world, above, below, around and everywhere, and altogether he continues to pervade with love-burdened thought, abounding, sublime, beyond measure, free from hatred and ill-will. ibid. 3,49

I undertook resolute effort, but my body was unquiet and uncalmed. Then I thought, what if I were to practise trance without breathing. And as I did so, there was a violent sound of winds coming out of my ears, like the blowing of a blacksmith's bellows. Then I thought, what if I still practise trance without breathing, so I stopped breathing in and out from mouth and nose and ears. And as I did so, violent winds disturbed my head, as if a strong man were to crush one's head with the sharp point of a sword.

By this severe mortification I did not attain to true knowledge and insight. Then I thought, perhaps there is another way to enlightenment. I sat under the cool shade of a tree and, free from sensual desires, free from evil thoughts, I attained and abode in the first stage of joy and pleasure, which is accompanied with reasoning and arises from seclusion.
Majjhima 1,242

Faith

By faith you shall be free and pass beyond the realm of death.
Sutta Nipata 1146

Faith is the best wealth for man. By faith the flood of rebirth is crossed.
ibid. 182

When one thinks that he has unwavering faith in the Buddha, the Doctrine and the Order, then he acquires knowledge of the Doctrine and the delight connected with the Doctrine.
Majjhima 1,38

The Doors of No More Death
are open for those who hear,
let them put forth their faith.
ibid. 1,242

What is the distinguishing mark of faith?
　It has tranquillity as distinguishing mark. When faith is

arising it vanquishes hindrances, and without these the
thought is clear, pure and serene. Milinda 34

Faith is to be understood like a water-clearing gem. As
water-plants disappear as soon as the water-clearing gem is
cast into the water, even so as faith arises the hindrances
are vanquished, and thought becomes clear, pure and
serene. ibid. 35

Leaping forward is a distinguishing mark of faith, just as an
earnest student of yoga leaps forward on seeing that the
minds of others are freed, and he performs yoga for the
mastery of the unmastered and the realisation of the
unrealised. ibid.

The flood is crossed by faith,
the sea is crossed by diligence,
ill is passed by vigour,
so one is cleansed by wisdom. Samyutta 1,214

The disciple Sariputta said: I have such faith in the Exalted
One, that I think there never has been, nor will there be,
nor is there now any other, whether recluse or priest, who
is greater and wiser than the Exalted One in the higher
wisdom of enlightenment.

So the venerable Sariputta made known his faith before
the Exalted One. Hence the title The Faith that Satisfied is
another name for his confession. Digha 3,99,116

Austerities

A naked ascetic came to the Exalted One and said, I have
heard that Gautama disparages all penance, and finds fault
with every one who lives a hard life.

The Buddha replied: If a man should go naked, and be of
loose habits, and lick his hands clean with his tongue, and

all other ascetic practices, if he does all this and does not practise the state of attainment in conduct, heart and intellect, then he is far from perfection.

But if he cultivates a heart of love that knows no anger or ill-will, and is free from intoxication, and delusions, and ignorance, and dwells in emancipation of heart and mind – while yet in this world he realises and knows that he is a true recluse. Digha 1,161-7

Another Wanderer said: We profess self-mortifying austerities and hold them to be essential, what faults are there?

The Buddha replied: One ascetic becomes complacent through the course that he follows. Another exalts himself and despises others. A third grows careless and becomes inebriated and infatuated. Another procures gifts, attention and fame. He makes distinction in foods, saying, This suits me, this does not suit me, and so rulers and their officials minister to him.

Now a disciple of the Buddha, teaching the Doctrine, does not lose his temper or bear enmity, he does not become hypocritical or deceitful or vain, he does not entertain evil wishes or become captive to them. The austerity of these things becomes genuinely pure, but it does not yet win the topmost rank or reach the pith.

One who is self-restrained, who injures no living thing, who does not take what is not given, who utters no lies, he advances upwards. Putting away the canker of ill-will, he abides with heart free from enmity, benevolent and compassionate towards every living thing. He lets his mind, filled with pity, pervade the world. This wins the topmost rank and reaches the pith. ibid. 3,45-50

Some men given to asceticism, living a hard life, are reborn, on the dissolution of the body, after death, into some unhappy, fallen state of woe. While others, living just so, are reborn into some happy state, or into a heavenly world.

But there is a way, there is a method, which if a man follow he will of himself both see and know the truth. It is the Noble Eightfold Path. ibid. 1,162-5

A monk is satisfied with sufficient robes to cherish his body, with sufficient food to keep his stomach going.

Wherever he goes he takes these with him, as a bird carries his wings with him wherever he flies. So it is that the monk is content.

ibid. 1,71

Miracles

There was a young householder who said to the Buddha: If the Exalted One were to command some brother to perform a mystic wonder by power surpassing that of ordinary men, then this country of ours would be much more devoted to him.

The Buddha replied: I do not give instruction to the brothers in this manner. Suppose a brother has mystic power, from being visible he becomes invisible, he passes through a wall as through air, he penetrates the solid ground as water, he walks on water as on solid ground, he travels through the sky like the birds, he touches the moon and the sun with his hand, he even reaches the heaven of the gods – and if some believer announces the fact to an unbeliever, the unbeliever might say that he does all this by the power of a lucky charm, might he not?

Yes, sir, he might.

Then it is because I perceive danger in the practice of mystic wonders, that I loathe and abhor them, and am ashamed of them.

Digha 1,211

Suppose also that a brother can read the heart, and feelings, and reasonings, and thoughts of others, and suppose he says, So and so is in your mind. You are thinking of such and such a matter. Thus and thus are your emotions. And if some believer announces the fact to an unbeliever, the unbeliever might say that he does all this by the power of a lucky charm, might he not?

Yes, sir, he might.

Then it is because I perceive danger in the practice of the wonder of manifestation, that I loathe and abhor it, and am ashamed of it.

ibid. 1,213

Another one said, I can see heavenly forms which are pleasant to behold and fitted to satisfy all one's desires. But I cannot hear heavenly sounds, do they exist or have they no existence?

The Buddha replied: They are real, those heavenly sounds. They are not things of nothing. By practising concentration of mind one may see heavenly sights and hear heavenly sounds.

But there are things higher and sweeter than that. By the complete destruction of the Three Bonds, delusions of self, doubt, and trust in the efficacy of good works and ceremonies, one becomes a converted man. That is a condition higher and sweeter, for the sake of which the brethren lead the religious life under me.

Is there then a path, a method for the realisation of these conditions?

Truly it is the Noble Eightfold Path. ibid. 1,153

Another one complained: The Exalted One works me no mystic wonders surpassing the power of ordinary men.

The Buddha replied: Have I ever said to you, Come, take me as your teacher, and I will work for you mystic wonders surpassing the power of ordinary men?

He replied: You have not, sir.

The Buddha said: Or have you ever said to me, Sir, I would fain take the Exalted One as my teacher, for he will work for me mystic wonders beyond the powers of ordinary men?

I have not, sir.

Then, if I said not the one, and you said not the other, you are a foolish man. Whether mystic wonders beyond the power of ordinary men are wrought, or whether they are not, the object for which I teach the Doctrine is this, that it leads to the destruction of suffering for the one who follows it. ibid. 3,3

After Death

There are some priests who indulge in the following speculation, The soul is perfectly happy and healthy after death.

So I asked them, Can you maintain that you yourselves have ever been perfectly happy for a whole night, or for a whole day, or even for half a night or day? And they answered, No.

Then I said, Have you ever heard the voices of gods who have realised rebirth in a perfectly happy world? And they answered, No.

That being so, does not the talk of these priests turn out to be without good ground?

It is just as if a man should say, How I long for and love the most beautiful woman in the land.

And people should ask him, This most beautiful woman, do you know what her name is, or her family name, or whether she is tall or short, or dark or fair, or in what village or city she dwells?

And if when so asked he answers, No; then the people will reply, So then you have not seen or known this beautiful woman for whom you long and love. Does not the talk of that man turn out to be witless talk?

Digha 1,192

Those priests who talk about the soul being perfectly happy and healthy after death are like a man who puts up a staircase in the place where four roads meet, to mount up by it on to the upper storey of a mansion.

Then people would say to him, This mansion, to mount up into which you are making this staircase, do you know whether it is in the east, or west, or south, or north? Whether it is high or low or of medium size?

And if when so asked he answers, No, then the people will reply, So then you are making a staircase to mount up into a mansion that you do not know of and have not seen. Does not the talk of that man turn out to be witless talk?

ibid. 1,194

Now I teach a doctrine that leads to the putting off of personality, so that if you walk according to that doctrine, the evil dispositions that you have acquired may be put away, the dispositions which lead to purification may increase, and one may continue to see face to face, and by himself come to realise the full perfection and grandeur of wisdom. Then there will be joy, and happiness and peace, and one will dwell at ease, in continual mindfulness and self-mastery.   ibid. 1,195

If there is another world, then the individual with the dissolution of the body after death will be born in a happy state in the world of heaven. Suppose there is no other world, yet an individual gets praised by the intelligent even in this life for holding right views and believing in the real.

But if there really is another world, the individual wins the lucky throw of the dice in both cases, as he gets the praise of the intelligent even in this life, and with the dissolution of the body after death he will be reborn in a happy state in the world of heaven.   Majjhima 1,401

Does one who has gained the truth live again after death? That is a matter on which I have expressed no opinion.
Digha 1,188

It is through the influence of Karma that the inhabitants of hell are not dissolved, though they are boiling in the fire for many thousands of years. For the Buddha said this: He does not end his karmic time until his wickedness is exhausted.   Milinda 68

Chief Gods

There comes a time when, sooner or later, after the lapse of a long, long period, this world-system passes away. Now there comes also a time when, sooner or later, this world-system begins to re-evolve. When this happens the Palace of Brahma appears, but it is empty.

Then some being or other, either because his span of years has passed, or his merit is exhausted, falls from the World of Radiance and comes to life in the Palace of Brahma. Then the one who is first reborn thinks thus to himself: I am Brahma, the Supreme One, the Mighty, the All-seeing, the Ruler, the Lord of all, the Maker, the Creator, the Chief of all, appointing to each his place, the Ancient of Days, the Father of all that are and are to be.

Digha 1,17

Where is that Great Brahma now?

We do not know where Brahma is, nor why Brahma is, nor whence. But when the signs of his coming appear, when the light arises, and the glory shines, then he will be manifest. For that is the portent of the manifestation of Brahma, when the light arises and the glory shines.

ibid 1,220

Brahma's religious life did not conduce to detachment, to passionlessness, to cessation of craving, to peace, to understanding, to insight of the higher stages on the Path, to Nirvana, but only to rebirth in the Brahma-world.

On the other hand my religious system conduces wholly and solely to detachment, to passionlessness, to cessation of craving, to peace, to understanding, to insight of the higher stages of the Path, to Nirvana. And that is the Noble Eightfold Path.

ibid. 2,251

The Lord, fully awakened, is the exalted One, abounding in goodness and wisdom, happy, with knowledge of the worlds, unsurpassed as a guide to mortals willing to be led, the teacher of gods and men, a blessed Buddha. He, by himself, thoroughly knows and sees, as it were, face to face this universe, including the world above of the gods, the Brahmas and the Maras, the world below with its priests and princes and peoples, and makes his knowledge known to others.

ibid. 1,87

The Buddha was staying in a cave near a village in the mountains, and a longing came over Sakra [Indra], the king of the gods, to visit the Exalted One. So he said to the

Thirty-three gods, How would it be if we were to go and visit the Exalted One? They replied, So be it, and good luck to you!

When he came, the Exalted One thought, This Sakra has lived a pure life for a long time, whatever question he may ask of me will be to good purpose and not frivolous, and what I answer he will quickly understand.

Thus invited, Sakra, the ruler of the gods, asked this question of the Exalted One, By what fetters are they bound, gods and men and spirits and whatever other classes of beings there may be?

The Exalted One answered, By the fetters of envy and selfishness, gods and men and spirits of whatever other classes there may be, are all bound. ibid. 2,263,276

Sakra asked, Are all recluses and priests perfectly proficient, perfectly saved, living the best life perfectly, have they attained the right ideal?

No, they are not all so.

Why, sir, are they not all so?

Only those recluses and priests who are set free through the entire destruction of craving; only they are living the best life and have attained the ideal.

Sakra replied, That is so, Exalted One, that is so, O Welcome One. I have got rid of doubt and am no longer puzzled.

Then Sakra, touching the earth with his hand to call it to witness, called aloud three times, Honour to the Exalted One, to the Supreme Buddha. ibid. 2,283-8

None of the priests, or their teachers, or their pupils, up to the seventh generation, has ever seen Brahma face to face.

It is just as when a string of blind men are clinging one to the other. Neither can the foremost see, nor can the middle one see, nor can the hindmost see. Even so the talk of the priests versed in their scriptures is but blind talk; the first does not see, nor does the middle one see, nor can the last see. So the talk of the priests versed in their scriptures turns out to be ridiculous, mere words, a vain and empty thing. ibid. 1, Tevijja

A sower does not sow a crop for herds of deer thinking that they will enjoy it and flourish long in good condition. But he sows the crop thinking that the deer will eat it and get careless so that he can do to them as he will. Some deer eat the crop and become captive. Others refuse it and plunge into the forest, but when grass and water give out they return to eat the sower's crop and are taken captive. Others are wily and eat the crop, but they are finally taken by stakes and snares. But others make a lair where the sower cannot come and they live in safety.

The sower is Mara, the deadly Tempter. The herds of deer are names for different classes of recluses, priests and monks. Some are entrapped by material things, and only those who refrain from their pleasures escape the mastery of Mara. One who abides in renunciation by wisdom has put a darkness round Mara and crossed beyond the entanglements of the world.

Majjhima 1,194

Sakra, the leader of the gods, is not released from birth, old age, death, sorrow, lamentation, misery, grief and despair; in short, he is not released from misery. But a priest who is a saint, who has lost all depravity, who has led the holy life, who has done what had to be done, who has laid aside the burden, who has achieved the supreme good, who has destroyed every fetter that binds him to existence, who is released by perfect knowledge, he is released from misery.

Anguttara 3,37

Decline and Renewal

The teachings of the Buddha are profound and of deep significance, bound up with the emptiness of this world. But the time will come when they will no longer be considered as things to be studied and mastered, but discourses spoken by profane people will be thought worthy of study.

Samyutta 2,267

Once a counterfeit Doctrine arises then the true Doctrine disappears. When foolish people arise they make the true Doctrine disappear.
ibid. 2,224

After many hundred years, many thousand years, men saw that the Celestial Wheel had sunk and slipped down from its place, and finally it disappeared.

Then there developed poverty, stealing, violence, murder, lying, evil speaking, and immorality. These things grew apace; incest, wanton greed and perverted lust; also lack of filial and religious piety. Human beings looked on each other as wild beasts, with swords to deprive each other of life. They lived in dens in the jungle, in holes in trees, or in mountain clefts, and lived on jungle roots and fruits.

Then this occurred to those people: because we had got into evil ways we have had this heavy loss of life. Let us therefore now do good, let us abstain from taking life. Let us do even more good, let us abstain from theft, adultery, lying, evil-speaking and ill-doing.

Then among such people there will arise a Wheel-turning King, ruling in righteousness and protector of his people. He will live in supremacy over all the earth, having conquered it not by the sword but by righteousness. Then there will arise an Exalted One named Maitreya, Fully Awakened, a guide to mortals, a teacher of gods and men, a Buddha even as I am now.
Digha 3,63-76

When this world-system passes away, beings have mostly been reborn in the World of Radiance, and there they dwell made of mind, feeding on joy, radiating light from themselves, traversing the air, continuing in glory, and thus they remain for a long long period of time.

When this world-system begins to re-evolve some being or other comes to life in the Palace of Brahma, and there also he lives made of mind, feeding on joy, radiating light from himself, traversing the air, continuing in glory, and thus he remains for a long long period of time.
ibid. 1,17

This was said by the Buddha when he was praising the special qualities of the Lord Maitreya. He will lead an

Order of monks numbering several thousands, even as I
now lead an Order of monks numbering several hundreds.

Digha 3,76; Milinda 159

Debates

There are the Eel-wrigglers, who when a question is put to
them resort to equivocation, to wriggling like eels.
Someone does not understand the good in its real nature,
nor the evil. And he thinks, I neither know the good nor
the evil, so were I to pronounce this to be good or that to be
evil, I might be influenced by my feelings, or desires, or
illwill, or resentment.

Fearing thus being wrong in expressing an opinion, he
resorts to eel-wriggling, to equivocation, and says, I do not
take it thus, I do not take it the other way. But I advance no
different opinions.

Digha 1,24-40

There are certain recluses and priests who are clever,
subtle, experienced in controversy, who are Hair-splitters.
They go about, one would think, breaking into pieces by
their cleverness the speculations of their adversaries.

And I went to them and said, As for those things on
which we do not agree, let us leave them alone. As to those
things on which we do agree, let the wise put questions
about them, ask for reasons as to them, talk them over,
with or to their teacher, with or to their fellow disciples.

ibid. 1,162

When kings are conversing they advance a proposition,
and order a punishment for whoever opposes it, saying,
Punish that fellow. Thus do kings converse.

When the wise are conversing, whether they become
entangled by their opponents' arguments, or extricate
themselves, whether they or their opponents are convicted
of error, whether their own superiority or that of their
opponents is established, nothing at all in this can make
them angry. Thus do the wise converse.

Milinda 28

There was a priest who thought of harbouring the following wicked opinion. Suppose that one has reached a good state of mind, then he should tell nobody else about it.

To him the Buddha said, The teacher who has himself attained teaches the Doctrine to others saying, This is good for you, this will make you happy.

Digha 1,224

There are things which are profound, difficult to realise, hard to understand, tranquillising, sweet, not to be grasped by mere logic, subtle, comprehensible only to the wise. These things the Buddha, having himself realised them and seen them face to face, has set forth.

ibid. 1,12

Ten Open Questions

A wandering mendicant asked the Buddha: Is the world eternal? Is this alone the truth and any other view mere folly?

The Buddha replied: That is a matter on which I have expressed no opinion.

The mendicant continued with the Ten Indeterminates or Open Questions:

Is the world not eternal?
Is the world finite?
Is the world infinite?
Is the soul the same as the body?
Is the soul one thing, and the body another?
Does one who has reached the truth live again after death?
Does he not live again after death?
Does he both live again, and not live again, after death?
Does he neither live again, nor not live again, after death?

To each question the Buddha made the same reply: That too is a matter on which I have expressed no opinion. That question is not profitable, it is not concerned with the Truth; it does not help to right conduct, or detachment, or purification from lusts, or tranquillity of heart; or to real knowledge, or to insight into the higher stages of the Way, or to Nirvana. Therefore I have expressed no opinion upon it.

The mendicant asked: Then what has the Buddha determined?

He replied: I have declared the fact of pain, the origin of pain, the cessation of pain, and the method by which one may reach the cessation of pain.

The mendicant replied: The words of your mouth are most excellent. It is as if one were to reveal what had been hidden, or point out the right road to him who had gone astray, or to bring light into the darkness. Even so the truth has been made known in many a figure by the Buddha, and therefore I go to him as my guide, to his Doctrine, and to his Order, as long as life endures.

Digha 1,187-202

Last Days

The Exalted One said to his disciple Ananda: I pray you, spread my couch between two trees, with its head to the north. I am weary and would lie down.

Then he said, These two trees are a mass of bloom with flowers out of season, and heavenly flowers and music come from the sky, in reverence for the successor of the Buddhas of old. But it is not thus that the Buddha is rightly honoured. The brother or sister who continually fulfils all the greater and lesser duties, who is correct in life and walks according to the precepts, he it is who rightly honours and reveres the Buddha.

Digha 2,137

Ananda asked: What are we to do with the remains of the Buddha?

He replied: Do not hinder yourselves by honouring the remains of the Buddha. Be zealous in your own behalf! Devote yourselves to your own good! Be earnest, be zealous, be intent on your own good!

ibid. 2,141

Ananda stood weeping at the thought, I remain but a learner, one who has yet to work out his own perfection. And the Master is about to pass away from me, he who is so kind!

Then the Buddha said: Do not let yourself be troubled, do not weep. Have I not already told you that it is in the very nature of all things most near and dear to us that we must divide ourselves from them? All things that are born contain within themselves the necessity of dissolution. For a long time you have been very near to me by words of love, kind and good. You have done well. Be earnest in effort, and you too shall be free from the intoxications of sensuality, individuality, delusion and ignorance.

ibid. 2,143

My time is ripe, my life will close,
I leave, and trust myself alone.
Be earnest, holy, full of thought,
Be resolute and watch your heart.
Who keeps the Doctrine and the Law
Shall cross life's sea and end all woes.

ibid. 2,120

Ananda said: Let not the Exalted One die in this little wattle-and-daub town, this branch township in the midst of the jungle. There are great cities such as Benares, Rajagaha and others, let the Exalted One die in one of them.

The Buddha replied: Say not so, Ananda. Say not that this is but a small wattle-and-daub town in the midst of the jungle. It was once a great city. Go and tell the elders of the town that in the last watch of this night, the final passing away of the Buddha will take place.

ibid. 2,146

A wanderer, who was not a believer, heard that the Buddha was dying, and he came to ask Ananda that he might see the Buddha and get rid of a feeling of uncertainty.

Ananda said: Enough, the Exalted One is weary. Do not trouble him.

The Buddha overheard this and said: Do not keep him out. Whatever he asks it is not to annoy me but from a desire for knowledge.

Then he told the wanderer: In whatsoever Doctrine and discipline the Noble Eightfold Path is found, there is found a man of true saintliness.

ibid. 2,149

The Buddha said: It may be that in some of you the thought may arise, The word of the Master is ended, we have no longer a teacher! But it is not thus that you should regard it. The Doctrine, and the rules of the Order, which I have set forth and laid down for you all, when I have gone let them be the Teacher to you.

ibid. 2,154

Then the Exalted One addressed the brethren and said: Behold I exhort you now: Decay is inherent in all composite things! Work out your salvation with diligence!

That was the last word of the Buddha.

ibid. 2,156

At the moment when the Exalted One passed away Ananda uttered this verse:

Then our hair stood on end,
Then there was distress,
The Supreme Buddha died
Endowed with all grace.

When the Exalted One died some of the brothers who were not yet free from the passions stretched out their arms and wept, and others fell to the ground, rolling to and fro in anguish at the thought, The Exalted One has died too soon. The Happy One has passed away too soon. The Light has gone out in the world too soon.

But those of the brothers who were free from the passions bore their grief calmly, and one of the elders exhorted the others saying, Enough, my brothers. Do not weep or lament. The Exalted One always declared to us that it is in the nature of all things near and dear to us that we must divide ourselves from them, leave them, and sever ourselves from them.

Whatever is born, brought into being, and organised, contains within itself the necessity for dissolution. All composite things are impermanent. It is not possible that they should not be dissolved. No such condition can exist.

Bow down with clasped hands.

It is hard indeed to meet a Buddha through hundreds of ages.

ibid. 2, 158, 167

From the Book of the Great Passing On, The Maha Pari-Nirvana Sutra.